Ink stains on a wooden bench

Rishubh Chakraborty

India | USA | UK

Presentation by *BookLeaf Publishing*

Web: www.bookleafpub.com

E-mail: info@bookleafpub.com

ISBN: 9789360942045

First edition 2024

To Babuji, Mummy, Ritu, Mani, Payal and Fluffy. The poem comprises my work, you have read and a few fresh ones!

To my English Teachers in St. Thomas' College, Dehradun and Holy Cross School, Agartala.

To authors like Ruskin Bond, Mulk Raj Anand, Enid Blyton, Shakespeare and P.G. Wodehouse

To Dehradun, my hometown and Mumbai, my safe haven in adulthood.

The poem seeks a lot of inspiration from nature—from majestic Himalayas to the honey bees; you have forever captured my awe and imagination and fueled a positive and consistent flow of energy, giving me the motivation to seek new poetic ventures.

Yours,

- the northernwhisperer

s/o Manas & Manasi Chakraborty

A pot of ink!

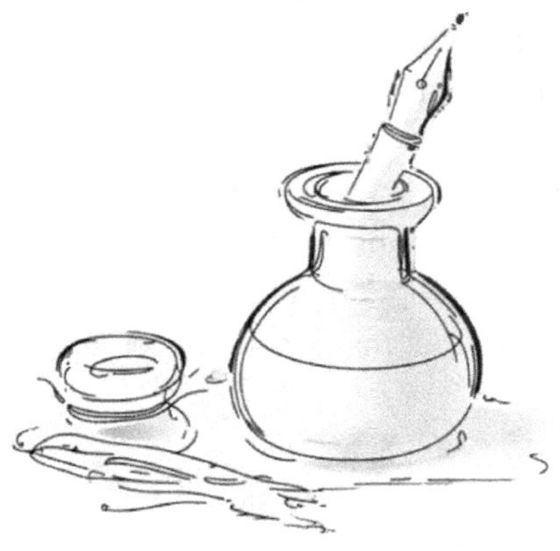

Hi, would you know,
Where can I find a bit of ink?
I'd like to pen a story,
That'd make you smile in a blink!

I know it's been a while,
That I scribbled on the paper.
Well, it's actually time,
That made me run around like a pauper!

Hey there,
Are you still reading this plea?
Well, come on then.
Get me some ink to let my soul free!

I'd love to get a bit lost;
Should I get obsessed again?
There was a time when
I'd escape the jungle to write about pain!

Well, not always, because
I'd also pour stories of deep love;
Tales of yearning, craving,
And recipes that make humans tough!

Hi, would you know,
Where can I find a fresh pot of ink?
Let me humour you then;
I've got a new idea brewing, I think!

A cup of latte, please!

There she sits,
Alone with her thoughts,
Letting the latte turn cold.
A few moons ago,
She was escorted amid a cold shower,
By a gentleman not so old.

Coffee and rain it was,
That got them to talk and share,
Only to colour the cafe in her laughter.
The vibe was certain,
And so was the sparkle in her eyes.
Did she find the one she was always after?

A night it was,
Sealed with a kiss and a hug,
But, she was ditched later and how!
Stirring the latte, aimlessly,
Reminiscing about the rain that night,
A shadow catches her eye now.

A gentleman, not so old,
Walks in with a lady, drenched in rain,
Rushing to order two lattes, on the go.
She catches a familiar scent;
Realisation strikes as she walks out.
Another girl will sit with a latte alone tomorrow.

Monsters

Hush for a while; don't you make any noise.
Gather yourselves all the little girls and little
boys.

What did your mama tell you before she went to
sleep?
Did she tell her love for you runs very deep?

A kiss on the forehead isn't going to keep them
away!
Stay awake—what if you woke up somewhere
far away?

Are you afraid of the dark and hope the lights
stay on?

But then, she did prepare you to be brave and
sleep alone!

Little angels, your hearts are pure and so blood
red.
It's feeding time—you never checked for
monsters under the bed!

Bookworm

It had been a while,
Since I saw you last.
But, I hadn't forgotten you,
My dear friend from the past.

I remember holding you close,
For the first time in school.
How I loved the smell of you;
People thought I was a fool!

I remember sleeping off at times,
With you on my side.
You showed me humour and drama.
There were moments I even cried!

It has been a while,
Since I flipped through your pages.
It's time to embrace you again,
And walk together a few more paces.

Flight to Calcutta

Today, my heart isn't in Mumbai.
I miss those old sweet shops selling
'Roshogolla'.

I have distinct memories of a charming city,
Where even the old men discussed football
during evening 'adda'.

Yes sir, this is the former British Capital.
A city full of literature, food, music and dance;
this is beautiful Calcutta.

I miss being the pampered grandson of my
Mum-mum,
And going to buy 'jalebi' and 'kachori' for snacks
with Ba.

How I wish I could relive my childhood days
again.
Maybe, sneak out with my aunt to watch movies
and hog 'phuchka'!

'Do you want something from there?', you asked
before boarding.
I wish you'd send me some pictures of the
yellow taxis and the majestic 'Howrah'!

Take me there, where you fly today, my dear.
I wish I was on that flight as well; flying to
Calcutta.

House for Sale

I saw a sign the other day.
It was a board on a lawn near the old cafe.

It was a 'House for Sale', I believe.
So Mr. & Mrs. Chatterjee moved out. That was
some relief!

I always liked the front lawn of this house.
So, I entered with hushed steps, like a curious
mouse.

The front door was left open; it was empty
inside.
I could only stare at the beautiful interior,
starry-eyed.

The empty hall felt so warm. It was indeed
welcoming.
But the house felt so lonely. It was really a
strange feeling.

Empty places have the loudest echoes, I heard.
So I screamed 'Hey!'
At the sound of my voice, I heard the house cry
'Would you, at least, stay?!'

Poet's dilemma

Have you ever had this thought?
How much time have you really got?

You and I are poets. Writing is all we really do.
Do you worry about your final poetry too?

What if you never woke up tomorrow?
What if you left everyone behind, in sorrow?

What would your last words be?
Would it be angst or romantic poetry?

Have you penned the words somewhere?
Is it going to be tough for you to share?

Would you leave the letter in a personal diary?
I wonder what your final words would
eventually be!

Monsoons

Let me teach you something about love, darling.
This is not the clichè kind. It has a different
feeling.

Close your eyes and open your ears.
Let it flow down your cheeks like precious tears.

Let this pure earthy smell intoxicate you.
You're about to fall in love and there is nothing
you can do.

Spread your arms and embrace this love of
nature.

Let it cuddle you tight as you melt into its
treasure.

Open your eyes and let this dim weather feed
your soul.
To make you one with Mother Nature, is my
only goal.

There is mud on the ground but don't let it
bother you, dear.
Darling, the season's first showers are here!

Heartbreaker

I remember the night,
Making merry around the bonfire.
Our souls were drunk,
And wine flowed to our heart's desire.

I remember the night,
As I clumsily picked up my guitar.
And at the strike of the right note,
Rose a blurred image of an unfamiliar dancer.

I remember the night,
When our eyes locked on each other.
As she swayed to the rhythm of the tune,
Circling perfectly around the bonfire.

I remember the night,
As we all eventually retired beneath the north
star.
Curious, I asked "Who are you?"
"One who'll break your heart". said the fiery
unfamiliar dancer.

Platform No. 2

The train pulled away from the station; I was
just a little late.
The next train was in half an hour and I decided
to wait.

Sitting on a lonely bench, something caught my
attention.
It was a pretty girl, sitting alone on a bench, at
the opposite station.

I was to travel to my left and her train would
take her right.
We couldn't help it but our eyes locked in, on
that beautiful summer night.

The clock paced with purpose and for two hours,
I was glued to the seat.
We both missed our trains that night; all I could
hear was my strong heartbeat.

What happens when you fall in love with a
stranger? What can you even do?
Well, I gave my heart away, that night, to the girl
on Platform No. 2.

Playground

Minister! You deserve the cheers now.
Elections are near and I hear you won't bow.

Ah! The promises of low taxes got applause.
I hear you put education policy on pause.

Oh! Do businessmen need better residences?
What about my security? I live without fences!

So, will there really be another shopping mall?
Guess, I'll bid farewell to the forest, after all.

I see! More factories do the economy good?
Wait! Will my brother grow old on processed
food?

You promised the world and begged for their
support.
If there isn't corruption, why do I feel I'm the
puppet?

I hear you take bribes; won't you change the
system?
Is this democracy? Certainly, not my definition
of freedom!

Minister! Looks like you've won this round.
But tell me, what about the children? Where is
their playground?!

Beautiful in Death

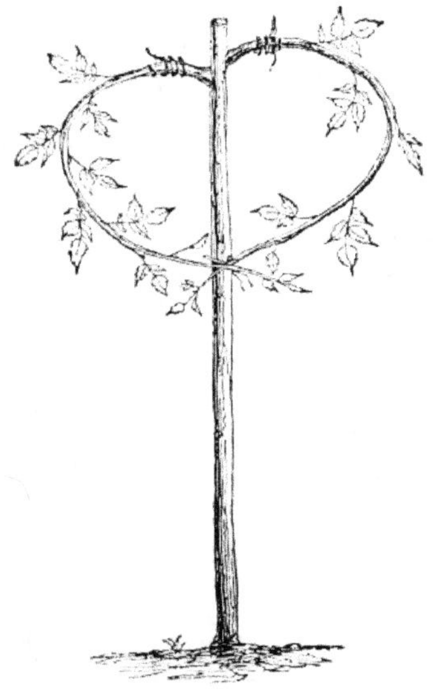

Listen now. I have a small wish to make.
Can you do this small favour, for my sake?

I wasn't a favourite child. I was useless in school
too.
I have failed my dreams. Yes, that is true.

The child within me has been dead for a while.
I discarded hope, since it was about time.

But I have a small wish. Will you fulfil this last
one?
Will you carry my ashes to the hill, when my
time here is done?

I wish to rest in the lap of Mussoorie, when I'm
gone.
Will you play John Denver for a while, when all
is done?

I want you to plant a rose stem on my ashes; I'd
be grateful.
I was insignificant when alive. In death, I hope
you find me beautiful.

Piggy Bank

Dad, have you seen my piggy bank here?
I want to hold it once; hold it near.

It has been twenty years since I last saw it.
You gave it to me on my birthday. It was a
precious gift.

I remember when you'd give me ten rupees each
week,
And mom would add another ten as her little
treat.

It was an innocent game; you taught me how to
save.
The few coins got me excited. Maybe, I was just
naive.

Life, now, is an infinite loop of a mundane
routine.
Only debt, loans, expenses thrived; dreams went
down the drain.

I wish life had more meaning than monthly
salaries.
We all look the same, talk the same—we are
corporate zombies!

Dad, have you seen that old piggy bank?
I wish to hold it and feel warm again; right now,
I feel a little blank.

Sun and the Moon

Do you think they are secret lovers? The Sun
and the Moon?
Let's not ridicule the idea so soon.

The Moon revolves around the Earth, right?
But the Sun lights her up in the night!

On rare occasions, don't they cast shadows on
each other?
Maybe they're meant to be together?

The Moon soothes the Earth, while the Sun
makes it warm and hot!
I would assume this is how they tease each
other. Or, maybe not.

On lonely nights, I wonder if they were
supposed to be one.

The Moon surely changes her shape, delicately,
at the glance of the Sun!

I Have

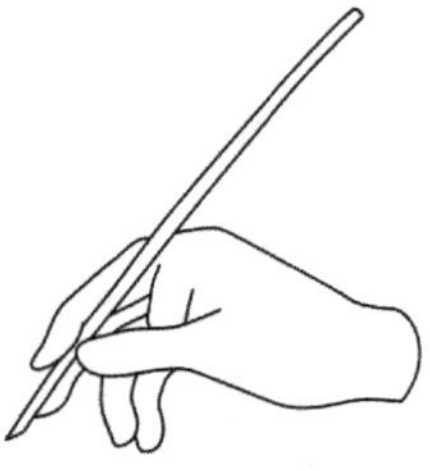

I have fallen and failed.
I have given and been robbed.
I have sacrificed and compromised.
I have bled, as I softly cried.

I have loved and loved again.
I have tasted the unimaginable pain.
I have scars and nothing else to gain.
I have lost everything but I'm still sane.

I have love and love alone now.
I have faith and I won't bow.
I have poetry left and you wonder how?
With ink in my veins, I'll conquer, I vow!

Cheeky Monsoon

Oh, you're here again!
You cheeky monsoon rain.

Oh, you make the sparrows chirpy!
But why do you make me so lazy?

Oh, the winds are so strong here.
How they mess up my long wavy hair!

Oh, it's the perfect time to indulge in a strong
coffee.
I wonder why I still feel so sleepy.

Oh, you do make me fall in love with you
always.
I'm addicted to the lightning and your
thunderous ways!

Oh, you're here again—
You cheeky monsoon rain!

One Time in Corbett

Ages ago, when I was a curious child,
My parents decided to take me to the wild.

I had half imagined myself to be 'Mowgli',
But 'Jungle' is a different experience really.

We were chased by a mama elephant once,
And we did see one too many peacocks' dance.

During safari, I was in awe of the lone tusker,
And how our mahout saved us from a young
tiger!

We were in awe to see a distant cousin of the
komodo,
Just as terrified we were when our camp was
attacked by a wild boar!

It was adventurous to climb the tall Machan
Tower,
Watching the deers enjoying their evening
shower.

At final dusk, as I absorbed the moment,
watching the calf play with mother deer,
I knew that nature was in balance now; we,
humans, didn't belong here.

Hello, Ruskin Bond

Did I tell you this story?
This happened when I went to Mussoorie.

It was a break from college and I was bored of
Doon.
A bunch of us decided to reach the hill by noon.

We were young kids trying to build memories,
Travelling the hill to collect our personal stories.

But, I had a plan; we took a detour.
On this day, I had to visit Landour.

You see, the writer within me wanted to meet his
idol.
Going to his house was no riddle.

He said "Hello" and I could only stutter.
Here I was, standing across the God of literature.

The conversations were about Doon and 'Rusty'.
The evening was about the old charm of our
favourite sleepy valley.

I still remember that small building, behind the
mist.
It was definitely one very special birthday gift.

The time is ripe again to hear the mountain song.
I pray I get to meet my idol again—Sir Ruskin
Bond.

Let's Talk

Let's talk.
I've a thought in my mind,
Would you listen—can you be so kind?

You're stuck for ages in traffic,
And you seem fine about it.
You've chosen a government to resolve
But they've asked you to forget it.

We have plans to build metros and bridges
And some ambitious wide roads.
We forget, it's us privileged few! There are far
more who starve; numbers run in crores.

You've made heroes of those who
Are supposed to work for us.
But you slave for them and fill their pockets,
As they thrive through a bloody nexus.

It's all a circus and all a lie—politicians, news
channels and everything in between.
They've divided you in caste, colour and God;
the nation has lost its sheen.

You'd sleep tonight in peace and wake
tomorrow,
To toil 9-5 in a corner of your office.
You'd earn peanuts and give away taxes,
To a system that will make you hope, pray and
wish!

Why do we need the rest of the country,
When we are crammed in just four metro cities?
This is where 'development' dwells while rest
Reel under unemployment and false sympathies.

When millions have to cover the distance
Only to earn their daily bread.
That's when you know that the system is
cracked.
What comes next, I only dread!

If you're a true democracy, why are you afraid to
question things of your will?
Who has forced fear upon you? If the country
goes down, who really will pay the bill?

Let's talk.
I've a thought in my mind,
Would you listen—can you be so kind?

For how long will we be turned away
From the reality around us?
Getting our fingers inked every 5 years.
Is that all this country deserves from us?

Bestseller

She was a fine one,
When she was young.
She would enchant many,
And there were many, who would cherish her
company.

She had many stories,
To tell the world and so she did.
She was explored by many through the ages;
Many fell for her and the stories within the
pages.

Old and wrinkled now,
She would patiently wait.
A hand touched her; excitement made her forget
her misery.
A young boy discovered her, in the 'bestseller'
shelf of the library.

Umbrella

Saw the little boy, sitting on the wooden bench,
Waiting for the rain to stop, as water crept
closer, inch by inch.

He was a bit scared and a little shy perhaps,
Watching the dark clouds pass the hill, in a
slowed time lapse.

I walked over to him, and gave him an umbrella,
A bit reluctant, he grabbed the umbrella
coyly—the young little goodfella.

I saw him get up from the bench, and check the
clouds cautiously.
Soon, he darted across the street, with his boots
chomping on the pavement vigorously.

As he faded into a blur, he turned back once to
look at me,
Passing a slight smile and wave, as I stood near
the bench with a half-drenched coffee.

Reminiscing on the old Mussoorie days, when
I'd be scared of rain and snow.
Watching the little boy with the umbrella that I
was once handed over, on the same bench,
decades ago.

Poetry by the dozen

It's raining in the bay;
How about some poetry by the window side?

Watch over the sea,
As you lose time of the tides that come by.

Let me bake some fresh poetry,
For you while you soak in the monsoon showers.

Fresh warm poetry out of the oven;
Keep a few for you and a little for the
neighbours.

Ah, the room is filled with the aroma,
While the rains sing loud, against the tin roof.

Here, take a bite of this poetry;
Relish 'em as the droplets hit you while you
stand aloof.

A little heavy, a little light,
I've baked one for each of you—tiny bites of
heaven.

Should I bake a few more poems?
Would you like them by the mood or by the
dozen?

Coffee Machine

Hi there, you are up early!
You seem to be in a rush—
Are you in some hurry?

Wait a little before you go.
You don't look the best;
You do need some coffee, you know!

Let me guess what kind.
Seems like an espresso shot;
Do you have something else on your mind?

Ah, you have a long day ahead, again?
I would recommend the black—
It will surely keep you sane!

But, you skipped your dinner last night.
Should I whip you a strong latte?
Coffee and milk for the belly, if you might.

Well, a tough week, it has been.
I am right here, to serve you fresh and hot;
Your best friend, the Coffee Machine!

Little Diva

There she goes again!
The little thunder, causing all the pain.
And now her mother flips;
Little diva has red, smeared all across her lips.

Look at her! There is nothing to stop little Tina!
There she goes again, dancing around like a
ballerina.
Isn't it cute how she dodges her mother?
But who can stop a hurricane like her?!

Is she posing in front of the big mirror,
Wearing sunglasses, a little too big - stolen from
her father?!
Look at her pretty little smile.
It can melt anyone's heart by a mile!

There goes our little fireball,
Covered in crayons, drawing on the bedroom
wall!
Look at her yawn now and get sleepy; such
relief for Ma and Pa!
She'd be a thunder again, come tomorrow; the
adorable little diva!

Blank Screen

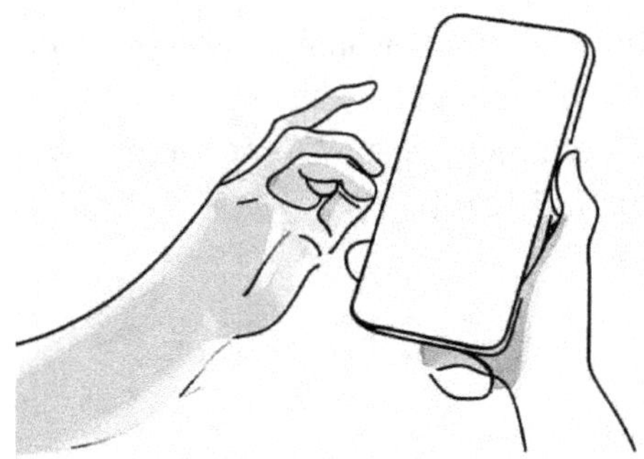

Coiled in a corner, he wanted to write her a romantic song.

Lying awake on the bed, she only stared at the silent phone.

How we wonder what the story could have been.

If it weren't the triumph of the blank screen!

Man-eater

Why can't I just kill the man instead?
Isn't he the one to clear the jungles to satiate his
greed?

Why should I not kill them then? That'd be fair.
I hide behind the bushes, with intense tension in
the air.

You may ask—what really happened right?
Well, an innocent tiger entered the village last
night!

It was a choice between making a kill or famish.
This was grim since the tiger had now tasted
human flesh.

The law of civilization commands death for the tiger now.
But we snatched their homes? When will the man bow?

I hear the leaves rustle. There it arrived, by the river bend.
My rifle aims at it. Our eyes lock; I hope the Jungle would understand.

I will never forget that look in my dear friend's eyes.
I am supposed to protect it. But the Jungle won't thrive until man dies.

Lead with the ink

The air was free to breathe,
And the water, free to drink.
The birds were free to fly,
And the animals, free to hunt.

There was nature on one end.
Man's ego on another.
One of them was massacred;
And we know who's guilty, I'd be blunt.

We've seen plenty of wars;
Something we didn't wish for.
Who'd save the planet then?
Armed with ink, it's time to lead from the front!

Burden of Dreams

I feel so tired now,
Dragging my feet on this hard ground.

Is there any way now,
To turn this cursed time around?

I don't remember now,
The moment when it all went wrong; it was a
long time ago, it seems.

I can't, any more now,
Carry this heavy luggage—the painful burden of
dead dreams.

Ink and the Paper

Do you think they judge me?
I hope not! It'd pinch me miserably.

I bet I heard them whispering one night.
But they wouldn't spread rumours about me,
right?

They do know all my terrible secrets and
fantasies.
Will they spill the beans and reveal the
embarrassing stories?

They do understand me; they know I'm moody.
But, sometimes I doubt their intent. Is there any
bond really?

I hope nothing changes; I love the three of us together!
But do they judge me now? The ink and the paper!

Love Letter

Darling, I wish I could write you a love letter.
I know I am a little flawed and a clumsy lover.

Don't you assume now that I never picked the
ink and the paper.
I failed to express; what word could express us
together?

I have been so lost in your moods and thoughts,
my dear.
You have mesmerised me just like the Pied
Piper.

I wish I could write you a song of our love for
one another.
You make me breathless, darling; how can I
overcome this stutter?

I love how you keep me warm even in the
harshest winter.
Darling, how I wish I could pour my heart on a
love letter!

Unpublished

You fell in love with the wordsmith,
For all the poems he wrote.

But do you have the courage
To read all the scribbled thoughts he once tore?

The Drawer

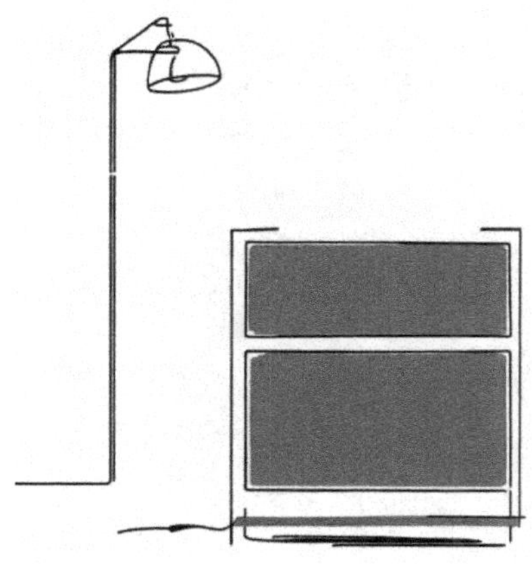

So, you think you know him well?
Did he share his secrets and what did he tell?

It was the charming smile, I guess.
His wicked ways have made you his mistress.

He is not to be trusted so easily.
Honest? Darling, you're mistaken deeply!

I saw you fall for his words and manners.
Pay heed before your naive heart shatters!

So you tell me, you know him well?
Did you know about them; angels that fell?

He has plans for you, just like he always does.
I know his intentions—even you'd cuss!

A gun and a body is his usual drill.
Darling, do check the table drawer—you're his
next kill.

One day

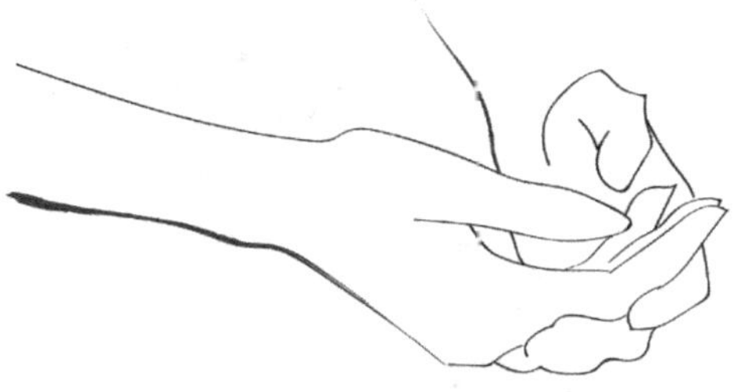

One day, we all will be fine.
No hate, no colour, no skin, no divide and no
war.

One day, we all will be fine.
No ego, no jealousy, no violence and no scar.

One day, we all will be fine.
No caste, no politics and no false Gods to pray.

One day, we all will be fine.
When we will be One and our ashes will be of
the same shade of grey.

Superheroes

Every dawn,
they wake up before all,
and work silently to prepare for your win.

After each battle,
they tend to you selflessly,
and help you refuel the fire within.

They see you grow,
from a seed to a flower,
and trade their lives for yours, void of excuse or
escape.

Superheroes exist in life,
much closer to us than we'd imagine.
Except, the ones at home don't wear a cape.

Secrets

Show me your scars,
And perhaps share your worst nightmares.

Tell me about your lies,
And tell me why you shed delicate tears.

Trust me as I also bare,
Hoping to get a glimpse of your soul within.

Can I also confide in you,
To take my secrets with you to the coffin?

Telephone

A decade ago, there was a phone call, in a tiny house in a sleepy town.

It was a girl and a boy, on each end—beginnings of a spark somewhere surely deep down.

Those were the days when telephones had long wires and emotions ran deep.

It was the same girl in his mind, whose voice had cast its charm and made him lose sleep.

Ten years passed by in a blink, and the attraction faded as if it were a mere game.

They say that the girl moved to a faraway town and pretty soon, the boy forgot her name.

Whilst they were gone, the telephone stayed on the same wooden shelf—in the house, by the bend.

Soon a little boy came along. Once again the telephone played cupid—the boy was hooked to the girl at the other end.

Balance

Do you think there is an accountant in heaven?
One who'd keep a check on the balance of heart
mend and heartbreak?

Do you think there is a balance in heaven?
For every heart that is liberated, another must be
at stake.

Mishti Doi

Let me tell you about a type of romance,
That exists only in the city of Kolkata.
A romance that is age-old and void of debate,
Surprising for a city known for its lust for *adda*.
This tiny tub of joy was a sneaky delight,
Managing to avoid a rift with the mighty
rasgulla.
Neatly, it settled itself on the busy shelves,
Adding to the 'gullak' of every mithaiwala.
While there was constant banter among
The older men around politics and dear Mamta,

Mishti Doi, the unassuming jaggery-infused
curd,
Soon became an irreplaceable delight, in every
Durga Puja.

Lipstick

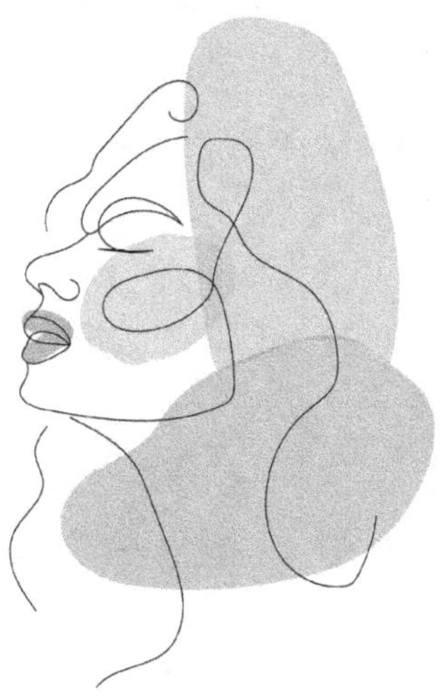

Hey there missie, I've got something to show!
Shades of red, to accent your natural glow.

I've a large selection to suit your mood for the
night;
Go for the light one or the deep red, if you
might!

Rushing to the school to teach the new
semester?
Here's a shade to suit you gracefully, dear
teacher.

Are you being pawned off to the government
employee?
Oh, you'd be a suitable bride. with the colour red
on lips and saree.

Wait, you've got a date now, have you?
Wear his favourite shade; would you have any
clue?

I'm sorry your man beats you up every other
day?
Here's one to hide the scar on your lips today.

Ah, you're late for your customer by the signal
now?
All these shades are for you, and they suit you
how!

Hey there Missie, I've got something to show!
Are there little girls in your lane, I should know?

Dehradun

Take me back to the days,
When I was young and innocent;
Where the wind had a song,
And the sun was bright in the morn.

Tell me again of the days,
When I was a little child;
A brat who was naive yet brave,
In a valley of hope, with nothing ever to crave.

Talk to me about the time,
When I first felt the warm fresh snowflake;
Or, let's revisit the days of simpler times,
When I'd break siesta with the melody of the
wind chimes.

Let's pack our bags to leave the chaos,
And rush back to childhood once more,
To have litchis under the northern stars and
moon;
It's been a desperately long time away from
home—my Dehradun.

The Laptop

Well, there was a time, sometime
Around my birthday,
When my dad suggested, I perhaps
Should buy a new laptop anyway.

The office was a rough affair,
As it always was then,
But dad was keen to distract me
To lift my mood and bring me out of my den.

I was a gadget freak, you see,
Dipping my toes into the new.
But, work had taken its toll on my mind,
Wondering if I'd ever get what was due.

After a lot of discussion, something
Did catch our attention!

A shiny Dell laptop, that could flip into a
tablet—
Definitely made for a great first impression.

It wasn't an ordinary laptop now;
Holding it made my heart jump.
A portal to a world of possibilities, it was.
Seeing it made me lose my grump.

In a long time now, I wasn't thinking about
Monday
And, its list of pending items.
I, now, held a tool, that ushered me back
To my childhood hobby of writing poems.

Writer's Block

Maybe, it's the writer's block,
That has me standing on the balcony,
Hoping to silently observe
Anything that could make for a good story.

Maybe, it's the laze,
That has me staring at the blank sheet,
Wondering if words would
Arrange themselves bit by bit.

Maybe, it's the weather,
That has been perpetually gloomy,
Making my thoughts wander
Away into memories, so dreamy.

Perhaps, it's just Sunday,
Begging me to ditch the ink,

For a while, to sit on my wooden bench,
To enjoy the Sunset, with a neat drink.

Hustle Bustle in the big city

Watch where you go, young lad!
This is no place to wander about alone.
People here wear many hats—everyone hustles
away since dawn.

Look out for the maids rushing away in their
saree, all stained and worn;
All the way to the celebrities' homes in Juhu, all
set in marble with a sprawling lawn!

This is a city that keeps the traders awake—will
their stock hit a high or plummet down?
Many migrants left behind familiar comforts;
many dreams have been carefully sown.

You'd think you'd get what you wish for; But
that'd be a miracle in the town.
The city lives are packed in metal boxes and
shipped daily on rails, south-bound.

This city is a paradox, bridging villages to the
bay, that's always on the verge of a meltdown.
There's struggle surely. But, there's also
Ganpati's blessings lifting the spirits, year-round.

The city serves rooms tiny, and dreams
big—nothing that you'd find in your hometown.
It will barter your soul for a slice of high; you'd
be trotting like a prince without a crown.

Houses on billboards command a premium,
that'd be yours at a 20% down.
But, the ones who run the show, serve the deep
pockets of entertainment in Goregaon.

Your feet will have to pace the race of time,
otherwise you'd be greeted with a frown.
This isn't a city but a circus—there are no
ringmasters; everyone plays the clown.

Simba

He was a brat, definitely spoiled,
Had a mother who religiously toiled.
He was a prince, in line for the crown,
His mischiefs did let his dad down.
He was stubborn and quick to rage;
He'd learn his lessons that'd turn the page.
He was oblivious to the twist in the story;
He'd encounter fate in his uncle, so scary.
He wasn't experienced to handle heartbreak.
His was a raw deal—a lot was now at stake.
He travelled far and wide to escape reality;
Had a hard lesson about mortality.

He watched as his guardian angel lay down.
He'd scream 'help' but no one was around.
He was scared when he felt a tremble.
His fate was to accept that life wasn't a fable.
He grew a recluse, as he wandered away.
His life was overcast—he was now a stray.
He travelled to seek deeper into the meaning,
Having learnt how to numb the feeling.
He discovered purpose on a dark night;
His dad's spirit advised him on what's right.
He ran back to his old life, to lead with intent,
Having understood, it was his kingdom to
defend.
He wasn't the young cub, anymore, in the vast
Savannah;
Having become courageous as his dad, the
mighty Mufasa.

The Banyan Tree

In a small remote town,
Somewhere in the north-east region,
Stood a tall, thick tree,
Unbothered by any season.

It had a purpose;
Purpose to spread smiles.
Settled in the vicinity were families,
Who had migrated miles.

The folks around were humble,
Unlike their children, so noisy.
Their curiosity almost always
Brought them to the Banyan Tree.

It had seen many families come,
And many, it had watched leave.
But, it always stood its ground;
There were many memories to weave.

While the fathers toiled at work,
The mothers did their chores.
But, it was the little ones who'd escape,
And visit the Banyan on their little toes.

Fascinated by the tree,
They'd often miss their classes.
All to swing and play on the hanging roots,
That protruded from the wide branches.

Often the families moved;
Their children, usually older now.
Soon they'd forget the tree,
That once centred their lives and how!

The houses, though, wouldn't be empty for long;
New faces would soon arrive in plenty.
Dutifully ready for kids to play, as always,
Will stand tall—The Banyan Tree.

Asylum

Don't you worry, li'l child,
Hold my hand and march back
To your bedroom—cover your ears now.

Those are black angels in the sky,
Whooshing like a shooting star.
What's all the violence, you wonder now?

Child, it's nothing but big boys,
Fighting for power, dressed in black suits.
They're our leaders and I wonder how.

It's a big, bad leader, who tried
To <u>put in</u> the military in your homeland;
There are bad wolves on the prowl.

Cover your ears and eyes child.
Momma and Daddy are out with guns;
No, they won't be on Zoom calls now.

They'd keep you safe li'l one.
This will be soon over. TV, Media, Politicians
Will nod to the same tune with a slight frown.

Hold my hand and let me sing to you
A lullaby of a land, so green and people, so
happy;
What will they call home, I also wonder now.

Wildflower

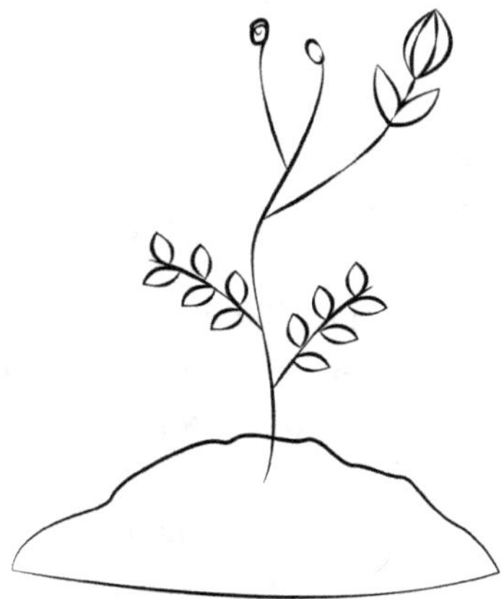

Strong gusts of winds
chip away the brick wall of dreams.

Heavy showers gush into
the dark alleys where the old Saint sleeps.

In the hope for some shelter,
all but one, scatter amid the thunderstorm.

Vacated homes stare into
the chaotic emptiness as the city gets torn.

Amid the chaos, lies one that dares,
standing like an unhindered tower.

Mangled with the fallen rose bush,
thrives the little wildflower.

Butcher

How can it be? She wears clothes so short!
Maybe she wants to get raped or maybe not.
She definitely has loose morals; has male
friends.
Well, maybe that is why you can't keep a grip on
your pants!
Yesterday, she returned after midnight;
Guess, society needs to set her right.
We heard, she goes out clubbing and likes
drinking!
She is definitely a slut. And, I believe in your
thinking.

So molest her! So what, if she has faith and goes
to church.
People will understand. They'll do the usual
candle march!
Once you're done with her, you will prey on
another.
That's alright. I'm sure you were taught well by
your mother.
I bet you will justify the rape by looking at her
'bold' picture.
Wait! Doesn't craving for flesh make you a sad,
petty butcher?

Why?

Why wouldn't the rain feel cosy anymore?
Maybe it's the grey; I wish I could have
childhood some more.

Why wouldn't the sun feel warm nowadays?
Maybe it's the old age; time does have its own
unique ways.

Why wouldn't the flowers smell as sweet now?
Maybe it's the city—a barren concrete jungle
and how!

Why wouldn't the stars twinkle as they once did?
Maybe it's the buildings behind which they all
hid.

Why wouldn't the sparrows chirp away in the
noon?
Maybe it's the clock; we are in a rush to be
somewhere soon.

Why wouldn't we go out to play outside like
before?
Maybe it's life; time once lost, leaves us on an
empty shore.

Teapot and the Cups

Once there was a teapot,
And two cups in a kitchen closet.

Oh, they were best of friends,
Goofing about from dawn till sunset.

The teapot would whistle away,
While the cups would sing together a duet.

How the teapot would serve tea,
As the cups would hunt for the last piece of
biscuit.

Well, there always seemed more room,
For someone to join this jolly riot!

And as they would merry away near the stove,
Arrived a brand new ceramic cup-set!

It approached the trio cautiously;
Elated to smell the aroma of boiling tea, you bet!

The Teapot poured some tea and spilled some,
Welcoming the new neighbour, a little too
excited.

Chattering away for the rest of the evening,
It was, now, 'housefull' in the closet!

Did you get me something?

On days he'd be out for tour,
I'd often wonder as a child.
Where does he go and why;
My imagination would run wild.

I was pretty naive then,
As a child can ever be.
But I'd look forward to his voice—
Bags of gifts would follow maybe!

My mother would lead the charge,
On days of his absence.
I'd often wonder why dad has to work;
Nothing ever made sense.

Well, for the naive child, that I was,
He was a source of toys and knowledge.
With him, I could quench my curiosity;
A taken-for-granted privilege.

It didn't matter if it was Vietnam,
Or if he had to travel to Dhaka.
There was a shiny new toy always,
If not new clothes for 'Puja'.

Once there was a video game console,
Where I first played Contra.
The other time, a set of green watch,
With a matching binocular and camera.

I remember when he got me the iPod,
As fondly as the red electric guitar.
Soon, he got a Bose speaker and Kindle,
Right after spoiling me with a Canon DSLR.

Every visit away,
Implied a bunch of gifts on his return.
Excited I was, as was my sister—
An insatiable pampered bunch!

Vivid are the memories,
Of hearing his familiar 'Hello'.
It was an announcement to gather,
Waiting for what was to follow.

Watching him unwind
Was always an impatient wait.
A Chai would always precede,
The moment we waited to celebrate.

Soon enough all of us would
Settle on the sofa—I'd be ready to spring!
My curiosity would best me usually;
With a sheepish glee, I'd blurt—'Did you bring
me something?'

Vacations in Dehra

I wish my piggy bank could suffice
To bring back the days of summer,
In my quaint, cosy home of Dehra,
Where we'd plot away vacation plans together.

Oh, how exciting it was then,
When we'd rack our brains for the vacation;
Indecisive, if we'd head to Naini or Dhanaulti.
Maybe, we'd explore a new hill station.

We had already visited Shimla many times,
And it was unlikely we'd go to Mussoorie.
Maybe, we'd again visit the hills of the South:
I remember when they were still a mystery.

Dad had an adventurous streak about him;
Mom, his ardent accomplice.
We'd spend hours hunched over a map,
Always slow to make any progress.

The bags were packed and the car was fueled up,
For the four of us to finally travel far.
Foggy plans would slowly clear up,
For a destination, not even on our radar!

The hills would call to us,
As would the warm beaches of Goa and Kerala.
We'd equally crave for Vaishno Devi trek,
As much as our nostalgic days of Agartala.

The adventure bug was perhaps acquired,
Or maybe it was just in our blood.
We could enjoy both luxury, and places
Where our feet were 6 inches in the mud.

What we learnt in Geography classes,
Was trumped by the experience of travel.
It was mesmerising when dad planned trips,
That traversed miles on the gravel!

We had savoured delectable Thai green,
As well as Betul's coconut-rich Xacuti.
We also relished the paneer pakodas,
on the hills before lunching at Dada Boudi.

We knew the mountains, or perhaps the beach,
Were waiting for us to visit,
As enthusiastically as the museums, temples,
And the wild jungle of the mighty Corbett.

It was vacation times, when we got busy
Trying to finally decide—it was such a privilege.
Will it be a trip across Roma and Interlaken,
Or perhaps, a quick weekend drive to Malshej?

Our travels could put Sindbad to shame;
Even challenge Columbus' spirit.
Well, it was always a getaway to remember,
Whenever vacations did pay us a visit.

I wish I had a coin to put into the slot,
To turn the wheels of fortune.
I'd be happy to go back to the vast Gir forest
Or perhaps, on a camel ride on a sandy dune!

Casio

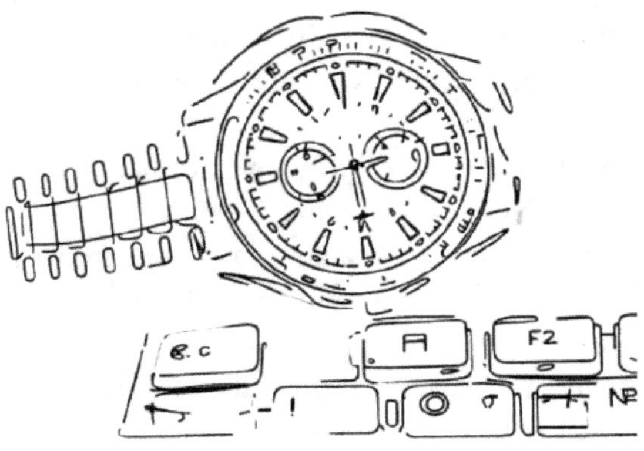

Tick, Tock, my favourite watch would go,
A gift, I remember, my father gifted years ago.

A tiny spring rung here and it'd flash the time,
With finesse—an engineering marvel, worth
every dime.

White dial, highlighted by a blue line;
Now, I had a shining piece of metal, that was
just mine.

It was a summer's day when I first saw it:
Obsessing over the watch soon became a habit.

It was indeed a gift, above a notch,
That left me toying, forever, with the stopwatch.

I haven't held anything, as special, I can assure;
A proud father, he was, at my graduation, I'm
sure.

A possession, I keep safe in the cupboard,
Only taking it out to adore, whenever I'm bored.

Sometimes I'd wonder—how it always looks
fresh and new;
A thoughtful gift by Dad—my shiny metallic
Casio.

Beloved Rose

Have you seen Mr. Vase lately?
He seems to be upset perpetually.
Is it because of the dandelions?
Maybe, it's because of Lily!

I wonder why he always seems so grumpy;
He used to be all colourful and happy!
Well, he's not been the same anymore,
Since beloved Rose left him, silly!

A room full of laughter

Darling, are the children home yet?
I'm planning to be home early!

Hope they have a good appetite today.
Perhaps, we can dine together, if there's no
hurry?

I heard the school was off tomorrow; is it?
Let me set up their favourite cartoon in a jiffy.

Well, I hear their laughter on the front lawn.
Bet, they'd be excited for some burgers and Tom
& Jerry!

Butter & Jam

There, they were at it again;
It was the same fight before school every time.
The butter and the jam were seen arguing,
Betting away their last dime!

The teapot watched over the stove,
As the bread tested the temperature of the pan.
Who would be the hero of today's tiffin?
No one could guess the mother's plan!

The butter smirked as it got spread on toast,
Watching jam churn in horror in the bottle.
The apple was neatly cut into the box,
Conveniently staying out of all the trouble.

But, the mother had a different plan—
She stuck a spoon to pick up the jam with
finesse.
The butter on one bread and jam on another,
Now stared down since they had unfinished
business.

Will the mother fold each toast separately?
Or, will she sandwich them together?
In a swift action, she slapped the two toasts into
one;
Jam and butter were forced to hug, much to
everyone's humour!

Under the floating stars

Mother, what are those lights?
Those are lights from the houses that light up
during the nights.

Who lives there and why is it in the sky?
That is a place called Mussoorie, just a few
miles shy.

But why don't I see the houses during the day?
Well, the clouds rise over the hill and hide the
houses away!

I also want to visit this place someday!
Maybe, if you study hard and eat your
vegetables everyday.

How will I ever reach there, though?
Well, there's a magic bus that you can ride and
go.

Can I get on the bus too?
Someday, yes! But Son, isn t it way past your
bedtime, at half past two?

I am mesmerised by the lights, mother!
Well, if you start sleeping early, we'll go there
together.

Mother, if I sleep early, will you take me there
soon?
Dear son, of course! The floating stars are hardly
any far from our sweet Doon!

Jungle Book

There he was, the little cub,
Looking meekly from the corner.
He was patient; slowly approaching,
Besides his resting father.

He wanted to practise,
Climbing onto tree branches.
But, he was young and afraid
To fall through the creases.

With one cautious paw,
He climbed on his father's strong legs.
This was his playground,
But the game was of high stakes.

Slowly climbing onto the feet,
With calculated and cautious gait,
The cub finally made it,
Without much await.

The father woke up soon,
Puzzled to see the little paws.
But, he understood the task and smiled,
After a brief pause.

He asked, "Son, are you trying to mimic
'Bagheera', the stealthy panther?"
"Well, today I'm Mowgli and
I'm running from the monkeys, father!"

I love you

The warmest smile,
And the sweetest smell.
Years of memories,
And many fond stories to tell.
The heart yearns,
Like a deep water well.
Thinking of you,
Makes the thumping chest swell.
The time went by,
Without pressing the doorbell.
I stood besides,
Slowly subsiding into a shell.
To go back in time,
I wish there was a spell.
The love within,
I never got a chance to yell.
At Balkum creek,
I, now, seek light at the end of the tunnel.

Life is, but a transient,
Rough sea conquering vessel.
To be or not to be,
We're now breathing Heisenberg's uncertainty
principle.
There'd always be space-time,
Where we'd forever dwell.